ANTHYMN

ANTHYMN

by Cosy Sheridan

Illustrated by Chad Niehaus

WILLIAM L BAUHAN, PUBLISHERS
DUBLIN NEW HAMPSHIRE
2006

Special thanks to
Jennifer Berman and Matt Minde
for the original CD artwork

ISBN: 087233-138-5

Library of Congress Cataloging-in-Publication Data
Sheridan, Cosy.
Anthymn / by Cosy Sheridan ; illustrated by Chad Niehaus.
p. cm.
ISBN 0-87233-138-5 (alk. paper)
I. Niehaus, Chad, ill. II. Title.

PS3619.H4633A85 2006
811'.54--dc22

2006036474

William L Bauhan, Publishers
P.O. Box 443
Dublin, NH 03444
877-832-3738
www.bauhanpublishing.com

To find out more about Cosy: www.cosysheridan.com
To see more of Chad's art: www.moabart.com

printed and bound in Canada

ANTHYMN

Six limousines pulled into my driveway
three were gray and three were black.

Six chauffeurs got out of six front doors
and opened six doors in the back.

And from each limousine came a part of a heart
like the kind you would see
on a card from Hallmark.

Each piece was carried by a family of ants
and on the lawn it looked like
each part of that heart danced

together to become

one.

I did not know what that heart might mean
why it arrived in six pieces in six limousines.

Limousines carry power,
ants usually do not.
Maybe in the ant world,
these ants were big shots.

The ants camped out with the heart
in the fine summer weather
and I watched as they slowly sewed it together.

For a while there it looked like Frankenstein
but a heart without some stitching is hard to find.

The limousines left, but the ants stayed

and each morning they circled the heart
and they prayed.
And they sang it ant hymns and ant lullabies
and the scars on that heart healed by and by.

One morning I looked out and the ants had gone
and the heart looked quite alone
out there on the lawn.

I went out to see,

I found a note there for me, it said:

the end

ANTHYMN was first born as a song.
Then it grew into a book.
You can find the song at www.cosysheridan.com

Cosy Sheridan is an award-winning songwriter, singer and performer. Her wryly insightful songs have been showcased everywhere from Carnegie Hall to the Dr. Demento Show. In addition to her many CDs released on the WindRiver/Folk Era and Waterbug labels, she has composed a cycle of songs for Robert Fulghum's book "Third Wish."

To find out more about Cosy: www.cosysheridan.com

Chad Niehaus is a professional artist in Moab, Utah. His evocative landscape art offers snapshots of the various moods of the American Southwest.

To see more of Chad's art: www.moabart.com